STEPHANIE STOKES

ELEGANT ROOMS THAT WORK

FANTASY AND FUNCTION IN INTERIOR DESIGN

with

JORGE S. ARANGO

Foreword by

XAVIER GUERRAND-HERMÈS

Principal photography by

MICHEL ARNAUD

RIZZOLI
NEW YORK

New York · Paris · London · Milan

First published in the
United States of America in 2013
by Rizzoli International Publications, Inc.
300 Park Avenue South
New York, New York 10010
www.rizzoliusa.com

Text copyright © 2013 Stephanie Stokes, Inc.
Principal photography copyright © 2013
Michel Arnaud

2013 2014 2015 2016 / 10 9 8 7 6 5 4 3 2 1

Printed in China

ISBN 13: 978-0-8478-4008-3
Library of Congress Control Number:
2012954522

Project Editor: Sandra Gilbert
Designer: Susi Oberhelman

The focal point of this elegant living
room is a beautiful family portrait by
George Innes. The painting's palette
informed the tones of the fabric choices.
I was lucky to find two Robert Adam
eighteenth-century mirrors from Hyde
Park Antiques in New York.

CONTENTS

FOREWORD

What a joy to be asked to write about Stephanie Stokes, a woman of great talent and wit, with boundless energy, a love of classic style, and a passion for creating interiors that place a premium on comfort. Over the many years of our dear friendship, she has helped me design perfect environments for myself not once, but three times.

In my first New York apartment, she designed an array of colorful rooms filled with Indonesian batiks, bronze sculptures, and French furniture—imbuing this modest-sized, light-filled flat with flair. A library was constructed from the hallway space, and a dining area was carved out of my kitchen. This became an ideal area to entertain family and friends. And I'll never forget that enchanting bedroom, with Hermès fabrics and orange details, which elicited a smile across my face every day I woke up there.

Our second collaboration was on a New York dream of an apartment near Sutton Place. Stephanie made the living room, which had a superb painted ceiling, so joyous and comfortable. For the dining room, she installed a collection of painted panels of flowers and birds that I had bought in the Marché Biron in Paris. This was a magical place to share a meal with friends. I had the best sound system one could imagine. The kitchen resembled a billiard room—everything was organized in such a way that made creating meals a pleasure.

For the third project, my apartment in Paris, which is chock-full of French furniture, I needed a dressing room that was incredibly efficient but could also accommodate my huge Syrian chest of drawers and collection of Orientalist porcelains and paintings. She achieved an incomparable mixture of style, elegance, and comfort for me.

We weren't always in agreement, and neither of us knew exactly where we were going with each new design. But through a lively exchange of ideas for each project, everything turned out for the best. And Stephanie is, unquestionably, the perfect interior designer for me.

Très amicalement,
XAVIER GUERRAND-HERMÈS

Xavier Guerrand-Hermès's *secretaire à abattant* displays a treasury of beautiful objects—from gilt Sphinx bookends and a statue of Napoleon to a lion-headed hilt.

INTRODUCTION

Clients bring designers their fantasies. They are mostly pages torn from magazines or pictures of hotel rooms. It's chaos. But creativity begins with chaos. It's my job to make sense of it all. Houses aren't just fantasies. They hold possessions. They have to be flexible. They have to be efficient and safe. They have to work.

Young clients especially have strong design ideas with little or no practical sense. They request white on white, even though they will soon be having children. They're going to want to give dinner parties. They're going to need a desk for a computer and a play area for children that isn't white. They will need an easy-to-use kitchen. Organizing and creating houses that are beautiful but also comfortable and functional is like playing a game of championship chess. You must think four moves ahead, keep your eye on the end goal, and be willing to make sacrifices to achieve that goal.

That game is not simply about storage, though to my mind, building good storage is an art. It has to do with arranging furniture in a way that works for the client's lifestyle and for various ages. It means providing lighting, drinks tables, and ottomans near reading chairs. It means creating oases of privacy and quiet, as well as flexible seating for groups. And it's about making rooms that are versatile enough to serve a variety of purposes.

Friends and clients have been urging me for years to do a book on the practical side of decorating. Surely, I thought, someone had already done that. But when I researched what was available, I discovered that very few books show examples of storage solutions or flexible room arrangements. And when they do, the storage area is shown closed so that its function is not apparent. Most of these books subtly (sometimes not so subtly) are trying to sell you specific storage products. Booksellers told me there was room for such a book about the kind of high-end work I do, which has earned me the honorary title of "closet queen."

What I've tried to accomplish here is to create a "beauty" book on chic storage and comfortable living, illustrated with photos of rooms that are practical and timeless, not trendy and faddish; workable and beautiful, not untouchable and precious. These rooms are, first and foremost, awe-inspiringly original and spiritually satisfying. I want my clients to call me, as one did, and say, "We're not going away for the weekend because we love these rooms so much we don't want to leave."

In my former New York City apartment, an enormous color field painting functioned as a backdrop for my collection of monochromatic Chinese vases. The ancient and the modern blended synchronistically.

More often than not, designers concentrate on style, or their "signature look," and forget practicality. To become a decorator requires innate spatial skills and color sense. Nobody should be allowed to decorate unless he or she can put together wooden jigsaw puzzles quickly. If they can't map out a floor plan that works efficiently or pair colors with dexterity, you can't teach them. Designers also need to know manufacturing and finance. Only about 10 percent of a designer's time is spent creating the design. The other 90 percent is spent making sure it gets done and deadlines are met. And this is the dirty little secret of decorating.

I appreciate that I have led a very full and blessed life with exceptional opportunities both personal and professional. Part of my childhood was spent in Colorado. When you grow up in that environment—fishing, camping, driving cattle on roundups, and cross-country skiing over mountain ranges—you learn to be organized about your possessions and you appreciate efficient design. I'm also probably the only designer who could rope and brand a heifer. From the age of ten, I was building and beading teepees and making my own furniture. I managed to talk the three little boys who lived in the neighborhood into wearing the Native American costumes I made for them, and I forced them to eat the dreadful meals I cooked on the open fire. Then we all slept in the teepee where, of course, each of us had our own little storage areas that doubled as pillows. So my obsession for creating "a place for everything" can be traced as far back as that, and it has influenced my sense of beauty, home, and comfort in one way or another ever since. It has to do with living in small places but still having big fantasies, and it's something I come by honestly.

When I was fourteen, my beloved Aunt Marcy opened my eyes to the world of fine arts, classical music, and literature. This thirst of knowledge for all things beautiful continued when I attended college in Virginia. On weekends I immersed myself in the intellectual and culture life of Washington, D.C. This eventually led me to a master's degree in art history from the Institute of Fine Arts at New York University.

Before becoming a professional decorator, I spent five years as an investment banker on Wall Street, which provided invaluable training for learning about both finance and meeting deadlines. After Wall Street, I traveled the world as a photojournalist, creating Pan Am's advertising posters and writing about topics ranging from the position of women in Japan to crocodiles in Papua New Guinea. Looking at the world through the lens of a camera teaches you many lessons about composition, color, and light.

My limitless curiosity about the world and its many wonders is a potent driving force for all aspects of my life. When I settled down and became a New York City decorator, I began to quiz clients about their lifestyles and fantasies. Nothing is too far out for me. All their aspirations seem valid because, in fact, I have traveled extensively, seen the world's great museums, and even climbed part way up Mount Everest and galloped a pony across the volcanic craters of Java. And still I have a list of many things I want to do and see.

Traditional decorating uses classic styles. Nearly everything you see in my former New York studio apartment is with me now but reupholstered and repurposed. You can rely on the timelessness of classics—they outlast the trends. In this baronial, 1000-square-foot space, I paired a sofa and an antique mirror and placed them in an 8-foot-long Renaissance Revival fireplace. Most of the furniture was covered in white fabrics to make the apartment appear larger.

To hide the bed from the living room area, I designed a room divider, which was composed of a series of cabinets for clothing. The opposite side was the perfect place to hang a painting. This partial divider allowed light from the 35 running feet of windows to illuminate the entire apartment.

These myriad experiences and adventures served me especially well when I moved to a studio apartment in Manhattan's East sixties. This apartment measured 1,000 square feet, had 14-foot vaulted Gothic ceilings, and 35 feet of glass French doors opening onto a garden. It was said to be one of the most beautiful spaces in New York City. Why settle for living in a sterile box when you can have an 8-foot-wide fireplace, hand-carved bookcases, and vaulted ceilings? To make the space livable, I built complex cabinets in the kitchen and bath and walls of closets in the bedroom area. I became obsessed with using every cubic quarter inch. One morning I remember rolling over in bed and discovering two unused inches of space between an arched wall and a cabinet. "Aha!" I thought. "Perfect for jewelry." And that is how I invented my pullout drawers for necklaces and earrings. The only place I could hang evening dresses was in a 4-inch-deep space behind my bed hangings. A photograph of this "closet" was published in a full-page spread on my apartment in the *New York Times* in 1987. To this day, people come up to me and ask, "Do you still have your evening dresses behind your bed hangings?" The answer is no, but the question lives on.

After twenty years, I moved to a grown-up Park Avenue apartment. But that first studio was an invaluable training ground for me. When I relocated to Park Avenue, I applied that maniacal quarter-inch precision to everything. Today, there are three crown moldings that are hidden jewelry drawers, and I have endless secret compartments. The only problem is sometimes I forget where I put certain pieces. But at least I know where to look. Behind every curtain there are cabinets with touch latches to hold vases or candlesticks. My 48-square-foot kitchen would be a closet in Texas, but we have served dinner for seventy people out of it; caterers say that because of its haute logic, it is an easier space to work in than most large kitchens.

There is beauty in function. Contemporary life is so hectic. Young people today travel constantly and look at computer screens all day. They're besieged with images. To them, elegance is not a gold gilt chair or a marble statue. Elegance is convenience, simplicity, and privacy. Elegance is what they find in a pared-down hotel room. There is beauty in having a closet so well organized that you can dress quickly with no frantic searches. Saving time is a form of beauty. Simplicity equals beauty—as does comfort.

I hope you glean many ideas from the following pages and that you will discover you really don't have to sacrifice beauty and comfort to make your home fantastically functional.

STEPHANIE STOKES

A similar photograph to this one of my bed appeared in the *New York Times*. It showcases my solution for storing long dresses. Such early lessons in maximizing space were and still are invaluable to me.

LIVING ROOMS

[COMFORT]

Speaking about the concept of comfort in his book *Home: A Short History of an Idea*, Witold Rybczynski, one of my favorite authors, postulates that "an easy chair had to be preceded by a desire for an easy posture." That desire arose in eighteenth-century France and has increased exponentially since then. In America, it became an art. Today, there is no more comfortable living room than an American one. Famously, Eleanor Roosevelt furnished her house according to the seating she found most comfortable; style was beside the point. • While comfort is still what we expect living rooms to provide, the twenty-first century concept of "comfort" encompasses many more attributes: domesticity, intimacy, privacy, leisure, entertainment, visual pleasure, and ease of use. Today's living room should offer a place to read as well as entertain, a corner where two people can have an intimate chat, a place that provides flexible seating, and a variety of areas that suit the needs of different kinds of gatherings.

RETHINKING AN
HISTORICAL HOTEL

The Plaza Hotel, a world-renowned landmark, is its own address. If, say, you were in Qatar and were asked where you lived and you answered, "The Plaza," you wouldn't need to add "in New York." Imagine, then, taking this classic 1907 hotel and converting it into a twenty-first-century apartment house. That's what was done with this legendary hotel that has hosted everyone from international royalty to movie stars and robber barons. It was no mean feat. Today's lifestyle needs have changed radically. Now the trend is large bathrooms instead of the original "water closet." In those days, people had a modest number of dresses and shoes. Today, wardrobes and dressing rooms can be vast. And certainly there were no sound systems, computers, or electronics to incorporate into interiors either.

Consider that when the Plaza was built, if there was a fire, horse-drawn wagons dragged barrels of water to extinguish it. The richer you were, the more you coveted a lower, safer floor. The developers gave the lower floors higher ceilings (12 or 14 feet). The top floors were reserved for servants and had only 8-foot ceilings. So remember that fact when you read that some billionaire has bought a penthouse for tens of millions of dollars. It just means he bought the servants' quarters with skylights pushed into the ceiling! My clients recognized this when they bought a pied-à-terre with 14-foot ceilings on a lower floor, which offered beautiful views of Central Park, horse-drawn carriages, and the Metropolitan Club.

This apartment desperately needed some humanizing tricks in order to make it feel comfortable for a family with three young children. The problem was akin to making a cozy space out of a barn. Because the developer of the Plaza had combined many rooms in the original plan, creating what looked like a huge ballroom, everything had to be overscaled—furniture, art, lighting—to balance the proportions of the room. By breaking up the "great room" into distinct living room and dining room spaces, and then by subdividing the living room into smaller conversation areas, the room now seats almost twenty but still feels intimate for just two.

All the art in the apartment has a sense of the ephemeral. A room this big calls for enormous paintings. One night I met artist Bill Jacklin at a Royal Academy dinner and fell in love with his work. When I enthusiastically told my client about Bill, she immediately purchased a diptych of a bridge in Venice from the Marlborough Gallery—the two images painted perhaps 20 minutes apart transmit a sense of shifting light. It looks perfect above the living room sofa and is reflected in the Swedish mirror on the opposite wall.

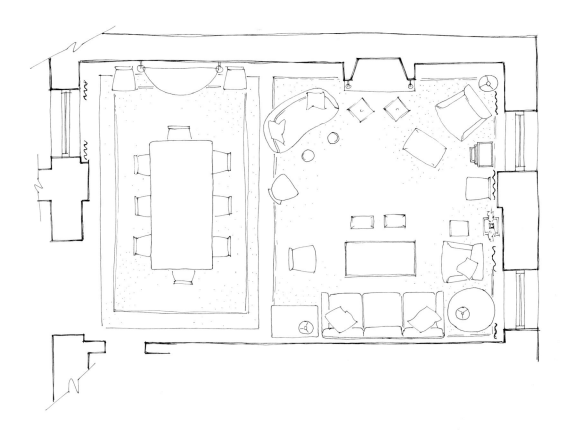

The main room measures about 30 feet long and 20 feet wide, so the first thing we did was to break it up into two spaces—a living room and a dining room (above). Two rugs custom-made by Beauvais clearly delineate each area. This is an easy technique to remember for modern buildings that utilize a "great room" concept. The living room is centered on the fireplace; the dining room is opposite the kitchen. The entire "great room" is coated with artisanal plaster by Art in Construction.

There are three conversation areas in the living room (left), the first being a main sofa with two benches and two chairs that seat about seven. Second, the husband's reading chair, with an ottoman, sits by the opposite window. With its adjacent seating, it can accommodate another three people. Finally, a love seat with two benches seats an additional six. Because of these smaller, intimate spaces within the larger space, you wouldn't think it's set up for sixteen to twenty people.

The turn-of-the-century Plaza Hotel was designed with 14-foot ceilings and dramatic, oversized windows overlooking the park. We decorated the windows here with curtains made of a heavyweight woven cotton fabric, which were fabricated by Albert Menin. Penn & Fletcher appliquéd a decorative pattern about a foot wide on the edge. This gives scale to the curtains. We layered in extra protection from the sun with motorized sunscreens behind the curtains.

Every view of a room should be a reward for the eye. This gold bust with an imaginative headdress of butterflies by Manolo Valdés from the Marlborough Gallery has a place of prominence in the room (above).

A large coffee table is essential when you have a family or love to entertain (right). This one is particularly efficient because of its two tiers. Everything on the top surface can be placed underneath when you serve hors d'oeuvres to guests. Who would guess that this indestructible, deep and rich finish is sprayed car lacquer? The Holly Hunt iron benches are heavy so that the children can't turn them over when they're roughhousing. The same goes for the two stone garden stools near the love seat (page 22). We chose small chairs to remove the temptation to jump on the "adult" furniture. While these are simple childproofing tricks, they're elegant enough that you don't walk into this room and say, "Oh, this is a childproofed room."

We custom-made extremely comfortable dining room chairs with curved backs and seats, and Schneller & Sons upholstered them in Ultrasuede, a fabric that can be washed. We added handles on each chair back to further reduce the chances of their getting dirty. A massive custom-built serving table with a marble top (7½ feet long and 26 inches deep) is filled with supplies for entertaining, putting them as close to where they will be used as possible. Overhead is a billiard table fixture, which antiques dealer Howard Kaplan fitted with string shades lined in orange silk to create a lovely, warm glow.

CONTEMPORARY CLASSIC

My living room is only 19 feet by 24 feet, not much space to house four seating areas and a breakfast table. It has to accommodate cocktail parties as well as conversations for two. My approach is essentially a modern one: eliminate unnecessary window treatments and adopt a monochromatic palette with one or two shots of color to punch it up. I've done that here within a traditional context. People come in and say, "Wow! What a beautiful room!" The reason they react so favorably is because, fundamentally, it's a pretty room with wonderful artwork and soft seating. Then they ask, "Why no curtains?" The answer is because I don't need privacy in my living room. And at night the view of Manhattan's skyline is beautiful.

As you enter the living room from the front hall, you pass a marble-topped cabinet with decorative grill doors beneath a haunting image of a Southern California landscape (opposite). Of course, this cabinet holds things. The drawer is home to various serving utensils, and the cabinet underneath contains candles and vases (right). It is purposefully placed next to the entrance to the dining room to keep these items handy.

Most of the furniture I own serves several purposes. On top of this Regency sofa table, besides a lamp, is a collection of ivory and silver tools—including architectural drafting implements—from all over the world. The drawers are filled with various pairs of those reading glasses one is forever losing. A nineteenth-century painting of a fjord by Norwegian artist Adelsteen Normann hangs above the sofa.

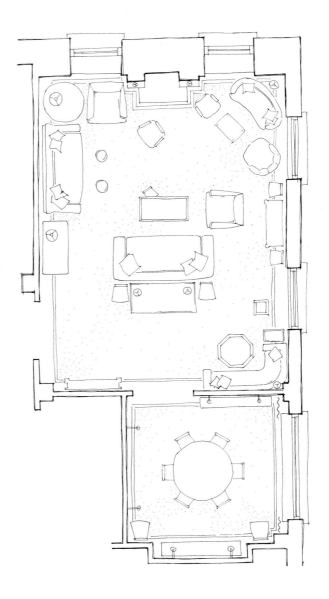

I love to entertain so I designed my living room to be comfortable for two or twenty. I divided the space into four seating areas, as illustrated in the floor plan above. The first centers on the white marble Regency mantle, which was scaled down to fit the room (overleaf). The focal point is the George II parcel-gilt mirror above the mantle. On cold winter nights guests gravitate to the goose-down sofa opposite the fireplace. The second seating area, which is in the far right corner, has the best view of not only the entire room but also the dining room and entry. This vantage point gives the illusion that the living room is much larger than it actually is. To the left is a third seating area. Above this very comfortable sofa is a painting of a Norwegian fjord, which helps "blow a hole" in the mustard-colored plaster walls (left). A sage-green corner banquette comprises the fourth seating area.

The sofas and club chairs are upholstered in subtle fabrics, which help disguise their considerable scale. Using two fabrics with similar hues is a basic decorating trick. The room's calm color scheme is punched up by gilt Directoire fauteuils upholstered in fuchsia silk velvet.

There are no window treatments or trim in this room. Who needs all that fabric to block the view? Two Directoire gilt fauteuils covered in fuchsia silk velvet can be pulled up to various seating areas. Notice that cocktail table surfaces in this room are either brass Jardinières from Florian Papp or a marble cut-down Swedish console, also from Florian Papp. Why? Because comfort also equals practicality; you don't need to worry about moisture rings on brass or marble. To the right of the fireplace is a tufted love seat with two chairs and a variety of movable seating. There is a small upholstered bench that can serve as a footrest and three Napoleon III low chairs. Designers refer to the latter as "floaters" because they can be easily pulled over to expand any conversation area. Firewood is stored in a former radiator cabinet to the left of the fireplace.

A *secrétaire à abattant* is, arguably, one of the most elegant storage solutions ever invented (left). With the desktop closed, it has a tall, trim, unobtrusive silhouette. When the desktop is down, you have an instant desk above which the cabinetmaker has provided eight drawers and two shelves, wonderful for stationery storage. Three drawers hold—what else?— more table linens (if you've read the section on my dining room, you'll understand what I'm talking about).

The remaining corner of the living room is where I have breakfast and work on my computer (opposite). Many clients ask for a copy of my high-low banquette. Actually, it's tricky to make. You have to buy two sofa frames—one with a low back and one with a higher one—and cut them down and join them with a curved line, which the frame maker replicates. Above the banquette I hung four paintings of interiors by the late artist Robert Moore. To the left, the marble pedestal and urn serve a dual function: they help visually segregate the corner from the rest of the living room, giving it a "just us" sense of privacy. Their placement follows a precept of feng shui: an open window should always have something in front of it that brings you back into a room; otherwise energy flows out the window.

AFRICAN AMERICAN ART COLLECTION

Before I met these clients, they were a hip, young African American couple who loved the party circuit and disco. By the time we started designing their apartment, they'd had two children and their lives revolved around playgroups, board meetings, shopping for bulk goods at Costco, and vacations at the beach. In other words, they were in need of a grown-up apartment. They had started collecting art by contemporary African American artists, which they would juxtapose with indigenous African sculpture and artifacts bought on vacation. A fairly neutral backdrop was required so that no one would come in and say, "I love your sofa!" Instead, they would rightly notice the art first, which I helped assemble with consultant Suzanne Randolph, a specialist in this area. Although I have an M.A. from the Institute of Fine Arts in New York and have put together several collections for clients, I wouldn't have had access to the studios and the world of top African American painters without her.

The mantel, original to the apartment, is the focal point of the living room (opposite). Over it we placed a circa 1650 painted Italian mirror—sophisticated, but not overly formal, with only a touch of gilt. The chandelier reflected in the mirror is Fortuny, from Odegard. The mantel is used to display pieces including a ceremonial African sculpture from Andrew Martin's showroom on the left and a piece of Kufic money from Tucker Robbins's showroom on the right. These pieces compliment the sculpture of a seated girl the couple purchased on their honeymoon.

The calm golden beige of the walls glows in the sunlight that fills the south-facing apartment and creates a neutral backdrop for art and furnishings—an Arts and Crafts coffee table, iron Giacometti lamps atop a Regency sofa table, and upholstered pieces. A custom sofa, Bridgewater chair, and a tufted tub chair were covered in traditional unpatterned fabrics. The Stark carpet adds a bit of subtle tone-on-tone pattern, but not enough to be distracting.

Behind the Bridgewater chair is *Azure Suggestion* (2006) by Frank Wimberley, an abstract expressionist painter known for the depth of space in his paintings. He creates this depth with layer upon layer of thickly applied pigments worked with a palette knife. It provides a bold, modern contrast to the more classical furnishings in the room.

Since this couple has a busy social life, we designed three conversation areas in the living room, all of them centered around the fireplace. This arrangement enables intimate seating for two or three people as well as seating for larger gatherings, with all the furniture facing a focal point where a speaker might be. To the right of the fireplace are two William Switzer leather-covered fauteuils and another custom sofa, as well as two marble-topped iron tables that can be moved as needed. The recessed shelves display African artifacts, most of them acquired from Tucker Robbins (opposite). The focal point of the wall above the sofa is Allie McGhee's painting, *Nu Vision* (2002), which depicts the rhythms of nature.

Hook and Ladder (2000), a painting by William T. Williams (right), is arguably the most important artwork in the room. Williams's paintings are represented in major museum collections. He is also the first contemporary African American artist to be featured in *The History of Art,* J. W. Janson's encyclopedic survey. The painting hangs above a neoclassical console next to the entrance to the library.

The library is really an extension of the living room, which is why we include it here (right). To connect the two spaces, we used a slightly darker palette, upholstering the walls in camel Ultrasuede. A custom sofa with pillows of Kuba cloth nestles into a nook adorned with convex sunburst mirrors, which serve to amplify the room's available light and expand the space. A reproduction Thonet coffee table offers a perch for books and drinks.

Vintage James Van Der Zee photographs depicting life in Harlem during the Harlem Renaissance of the 1920s and '30s hang above a desk (above).

LIBRARIES

[READ, WORK, DRINK, PLAY, DREAM]

If you ask clients, "What's your favorite room in the house?" chances are they will reply, "The library." Why? Because people gravitate toward the inherent coziness of a library. For even the most serious techie there is nothing quite so comforting as a room with book-lined walls. Libraries tend to be small, comfortably cluttered, and more conducive to intimate conversation. • Libraries of yesteryear were private spaces for retreat and quiet contemplation, a concept that today seems old-fashioned. Today, libraries are poetic. They must function in a variety of ways. They may double as an office, guest room, bar, or media room. Often they can even double as dining rooms or entry rooms, or any combination thereof. • The problem with a library is when you add new books everything has to be rearranged. If anyone ever finds out the solution to this ongoing drama, can they please come over and reorganize mine? Every three years I find I have to get rid of a third of what has been accumulated or risk a Collyer Brothers–type situation with stacks of books everywhere.

ONE ROOM, FIVE FUNCTIONS

I never bought objects specifically for my library; I just unpacked what I had. It's my treasure chest gathered from a life of travel and adventures. I've taken a wildly free-form approach, assembling things that may not be perfect together but that are part of my life. Clearly it works, because people walk in, take a deep breath and say, "I just want to live in this room." Its appeal has to do with its eccentricities, which are many. And I think city dwellers in particular covet such a refuge, no matter how small.

I'm in love with Sir John Soane, the English neoclassical architect with a modern aesthetic. Inspired by Soane, I wanted this to be an eclectic room that reflected an eclectic life. With the help of an English architect, I designed a library with 10-foot-tall columns of books with shelves in between them for objects. The vertical accents make the ceiling appear higher. The craftsmanship is incredibly precise. There are no fillers in this library. The cabinetmaker was not off by an eighth of an inch. The blue-green color alludes to the medieval tapestries in the Cluny Museum in Paris, a memory from my days at the Sorbonne. The curtains are made from an Islamic-inspired textile designed by a best friend, the late Lady Victoria Waymouth of England.

I have been adding to the room ever since. Last year, for instance, I found an antique ikat in Uzbekistan and covered a 1950s American chair with it. While visiting Jordan and Samarkand, I purchased extraordinary hand-embroidered textiles that I had made into pillows. In the souk of Istanbul I came across irresistible tulips that were appliquéd onto silk velvet cushions for Egyptian Revival stools from Florian Papp. What I like about the botanical prints above the sofa is that they aren't pretty; they are gutsy. They depict cornhusks and beans, not irises and roses. I found the little brass tables by the fauteuils in Beirut. They are portable and come in handy all over the house. I converted two Japanese ritual candlesticks into lamps that sit on my grandmother's antique French desk. This is not your average room.

My personal *wunderkammer* gives me endless pleasure. The multipurpose library holds books, serves as a guest room, media room, wet bar, and a gift-wrapping station, and there is an adjoining guest bath, which includes a discreet closet for cleaning supplies. Now, it is also the office for my design business.

The book cases are illuminated with eleven custommade gooseneck light fixtures with heavy brass shells found in England (above). The trick was to create small brass back-plates that fit into the narrow Soanian woodwork.

One day I was in a cab near Pimlico Road in London and I screamed at the driver to stop because I had spotted some botanical prints at Mark Ransom (opposite). Hendrik van Rheede had created the prints in Malabar in 1680, and they are inscribed in Malay, Arabic, Sanskrit, and Latin. I bought them instantly, and they now hang above my sofa. The wooden deer from Bali on the shelves are believed to hold the spirits of ancestors. They remind me of my blissful year in Indonesia. The Coptic crosses on the side table are from Ethiopia.

The most important piece of furniture in the room is an English Regency side table, circa 1830 (opposite). I paired it with a small dressing table chair worth perhaps $75, which I covered with a remnant of French tapestry. Pillows from Jordan and from a mosque in Samarkand sit on the English chenille sleep sofa. The seating is rounded out by a Moroccan-style leather ottoman from Profiles and two Egyptian Revival stools with Turkish embroideries. This eclectic mix of furnishings works. Sliding pocket doors, 10 feet high, close the room off from the entry (left).

I converted the closet to the left of the library door into a wet bar with storage for more glasses than anyone needs in a lifetime. They're hidden behind cabinet doors covered in faux book spines, ordered from England, to make the cabinets look like shelves of books. Since 90 percent of my glassware resides in the bar, at parties it all ends up in the 18-inch-wide Miele dishwasher right below the glass cabinet. There is also an under-counter refrigerator for soft drinks and beer, and an icemaker. Additional storage was built for more sodas, sparkling water, and artifacts I pick up on my sojourns—Turcoman jewelry from Afghanistan, a Majapahit head, a Javanese mask, prayer boxes acquired while trekking in Ladakh, and prehistoric pottery from the Middle East. We built a surround of wine shelves to frame the bar. There are four drawers for more liquor as well as brandy and liqueurs.

This library is easily converted to a guest room (overleaf). Two comfortable French fauteuils upholstered in durable bouclé sit in front of the desk. At nighttime, I simply pull out the sofa bed and dress it with linens from a closet built into the millwork opposite it. Guests often ask me, "What's the address here? What's the phone number?" So I had Penn & Fletcher in Long Island City custom-embroider the bed linens with the phone and fax number and the address, as well as "Stephanie's Guest Room" on the turndown of the top sheet. A guest bath opens into the room.

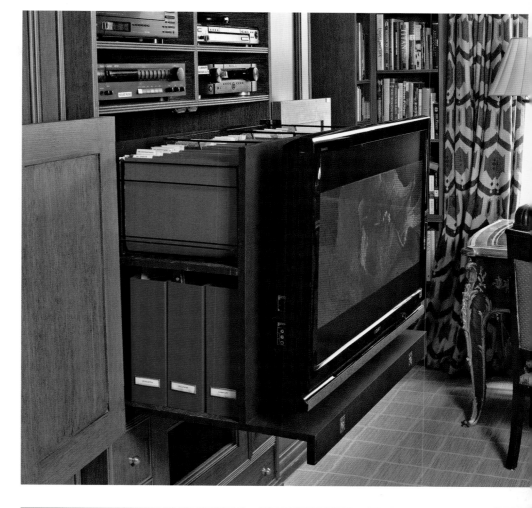

The cabinet across from the sofa contains shelves for audiovisual equipment. Below it, hidden behind cabinet doors, is the television. When we digitized my nine hundred CDs and swapped the big old clunker for a flat-screen television, it freed enough space to create compartments behind the screen for hanging files and office supplies. The load of files and supplies is so heavy that four sets of industrial glides were installed underneath the television platform, made by Rusk Renovations. Beneath are purpose-built drawers for CDs and DVDs. On the right, I converted one of the guest closets into a gift-wrapping station, with space above for linens. Guests use a closet to the left of the television. More storage is found above the television (overleaf). It holds electrical cords, computer wiring, paper products, tools, and more—all of it stashed into functional wire baskets in frames purchased from the Container Store.

TRADER'S WALNUT AT-HOME OFFICE

Home offices are not new. This one belongs to a trader who often works at home. As an office is all about storage, we designed plenty of open shelving for books and personal effects and, underneath, drawers and cabinets for files and supplies. The room had to be practical for meetings with business associates, but it also had to be a versatile and welcoming space for watching football and movies. The owner once told me he imagines suitors asking for the hands of his daughters here.

I built the entire room in walnut, the most beautiful of all woods. The quality of the millwork is exceptional. White-veined black marble on the fireplace, windowsill, and bar surfaces complements the walnut. The fireplace, with its Ionic pilasters, fluted hand-carved details, and recessed panels, displays the high level of craftsmanship of the woodwork.

A man's library should also be personalized beyond the made-to-order cabinetry. We carefully chose appropriate art, such as the maritime Adelsteen Normann painting behind the sofa. The owner is an avid sailor; the scene of boats gliding past impressive Norwegian fjords appeals to him. For comfort, we filled the room with seating upholstered in durable yet beautiful fabrics—leather, patterned weaves, and chenille. Because my client's four children also gather here to watch television or to study, I chose an indestructible carpet with a pattern woven in many colors from Stark.

There was one odd detail we needed to deal with. The space was not perfectly rectangular because it had two cut-off corners in the front of the room and another diagonally opposite in the back. Into the cut-off corner at the front of the room we installed a bar. The faux corner across from it became home to an ice maker, refrigerator, and extra storage. The trader's desk sits in front of the window between them.

CLUB RED

I was blessed with a client who had a wonderful sense of humor. She was looking for a library that had a shabby-chic, old English look, but she also wanted you to smile. Fortunately, she already owned many of the building blocks—specifically, an old leather tufted sofa, an Oriental rug, several odd chairs she was devoted to, and a collection of dog art and accessories. Aside from its informal, inviting aesthetic, the shabby-chic look also had a purely practical purpose. A gaggle of grandchildren often filled the room, so it needed to be easily maintained.

People either love or hate red libraries; no one is neutral. This may be because many American reds are brash and brittle. We chose a Pompeian red for the room because it has a certain fullness and depth. The strié glazed walls soften the room, avoiding the darkness a matte finish would have created. Red also goes well with Oriental rugs, especially Herizes.

How do you ensure that a room can handle rambunctious grandchildren? Easy: fill it with a forgiving proliferation of different patterns. The eye is so stimulated that it easily passes over any stains. We pulled our fabric palette from colors in the rug, then we covered the furniture with about a dozen different textiles, from plaid and florals to needlepoint and stripes. Since their colors all belong to the same group, the look is harmonious, rather than chaotic. A portrait of a Weimaraner in epaulets and naval togs takes center stage above the Chesterfield sofa. The sofa, by the way, was too low, so we raised it almost 6 inches on great big mahogany ball feet.

Since some people do more than just read in libraries, we needed a bar—in this case, a major bar. Cabinet doors carved and painted to look like rows of books conceal shelves of glassware, bar supplies, and spirits. Beneath them is a refrigerator for beverages and mixers. Additional cabinets hold more beverages. To the left is a television, also hidden behind cabinetry.

The devil is in the details, but so is the fun. The curtain rod finials reminded me of beehives, so we affixed little gold bees to them using thin, almost invisible wire. The bees appear to be buzzing around the hives. We selected various trims for the toss pillows to add layers of richness.

CLEAN, MODERN ELEGANCE

Here was a fun assignment for a family apartment: a room measuring 13 feet by 15 feet had to be skillfully fitted to serve not only as a library and media center but also as a bedroom for a boy who likes to invite friends for sleepovers. I used every space-expanding trick in the book on this one, starting with limiting the palette to just three colors: caramel, chartreuse, and neutral beige for the carpet. The result? A cozy, modern room that is at once fun and sophisticated.

Nowadays, libraries may not contain a single book. Instead, they house the Kindle, the Nook, the iPad. That may be the library of the future. But that doesn't mean that our approach to libraries, philosophically and aesthetically, has changed. There are no rules about libraries today save one: they still must be cozy and nurturing.

While the caramel lacquer makes the room rich, warm, and sophisticated, pops of chartreuse make it more kid-friendly and bright. By using both colors on club chairs—which we customized to smaller proportions—the room also feels more contemporary. All the art in the house has a sense of spiritual and physical depth. The James Casebere large-format photo above this vignette is a particularly good example. Not only is it mesmerizing but it also creates the illusion of the continuation of space beyond the physical wall.

The proportions weren't the only thing that was miniscule. The room had only one window, and because it faced a nearby building, it didn't admit much light. So the first order of business was to maximize the available light sources and increase them with reflective surfaces. That called for caramel-colored lacquer walls and a dozen French mirrors framed in seashells purchased from Maison Gerard in New York. Lacquer, mirrors, and the iridescence of the shells send light bouncing around the room. Oversized sconces (32 inches tall) add a hint of grand proportion. The sofa is upholstered in durable chenille (remember, this is also the boy's bedroom), but the chartreuse piping and the silk pillows add a tailored elegance more fitting for the room's adult users. Two small coffee tables can be moved when it's time to convert the sofa into a bed for the young boy.

A French modernist desk purchased from the Profiles showroom at the New York Design Center and a flat-screen above it fulfill the husband's work needs and the family's desire for a media room. Another terrific technique that creates a sense of a larger space is installing wall-to-wall carpeting (an area rug tends to minimize a space). Also, since furniture can stand both on and off an area rug, wall-to-wall carpeting makes it easier to vacuum the room.

Every library needs a comfortable reading chair with an upholstered ottoman and a great reading lamp in a cozy corner for refuge (opposite). The painting that hangs over the reading chair is a 1940s French abstraction from BK Antiques.

DINING ROOMS

I think of dining rooms as theaters. They are stage sets for dinners with table settings as decoration. It is important to have all those props—centerpieces, napkins, candlesticks, salts and peppers—close at hand. This means providing storage that matches the elegance of the room. A dining room must also be atmospheric, alluring, mysterious, and seductive. It needs to convey ceremony and ritual. The meal may take only an hour, but the experience of it should be sensual; that is, it should delight the senses—sight, smell, taste. People will remember the atmosphere and beauty of a room. • Dining rooms are mutable. You can alter the feel of the room dramatically by changing flowers, settings, and tablecloths. If you build such ideas into your dining room, even take-out can be transformed into a sublime experience.

LACQUERED NEOCLASSICAL STUNNER

In New York City, you may have a dining room as small as mine, which is a mere 11 feet by 12 feet. New Yorkers are nothing if not ingenious for their ability to squeeze astonishing utility out of even the most miniscule spaces.

And the truth is, I needed a dining room. I entertain a great deal, and I don't do it lightly. I am obsessive about setting a beautiful table. Wherever I travel, I am constantly buying linens, china, and tableware so I have more than enough to create whatever mood I wish. There are pastel settings for the spring and glittery gold settings for Christmas. I use faience plates from Apt for informal dinners. And here I have a confession to make: I own 126 tablecloths. Yes, it's an addiction, but when you're in Syria and you see an antique ikat or an artisanal cloth with glorious embroidery on burlap, why resist?

My dining room seats twelve very comfortably, thanks to a host of space-expanding sleights of hand. The table expands from 57 to 74 inches, and the twelve chairs were chosen not only for beauty and comfort but also for their ability to fit around the enlarged table.

The walls are lacquered in a taupe-gray paint from Fine Paints of Europe. Everything looks good against this backdrop. You can set the table with sunflowers one day, at Christmastime you can do it up in red carnations, and in spring you can use fuchsia peonies or tulips. Within these walls, the limited palette of golds, silvers, and blues provides a great ambience for any mood you desire. The powder-blue chairs are upholstered in resilient Ultrasuede. And what is that chandelier, you might ask? I found a woman in Italy hand-blowing glass blobs and shipped seventeen of them home with the idea of creating a fixture using LED lighting and fishing wire. It took nine months and nine artisans skilled in different trades, but this original chandelier gives the dining room a contemporary look. Lighting is extremely important. During the day, natural light bounces off all the reflective surfaces—mirrors, lacquered walls, and a ceiling covered in gold tea paper—making the room feel even bigger. At night, the crystal Regency sconces, updated with translucent gold organza shades, create a similar effect.

In my dining room, there's not a bad seat in the house. If you sit by the window, you look at a capriccio à la Giovanni Paolo Panini, which Thomas Stokes brought to America in 1784. It had been relegated to an attic. I took it to an art appraiser who turned to me and, in hushed tones, said, "What you have here is a Panini. You just became very, very rich." After some cleaning, however, it was determined to be an English copy. It doesn't matter. The painting is beautiful, and its panoramic views of classic Roman ruins pull you in. If you sit by the capriccio, you get views of Park Avenue.

If you sit with your back to the cabinet, you face another gilded mirror. The two mirrors reflect each other, visually multiplying the space. The candles sparkle against multiple mirrors and lacquered walls. Dining here is magical.

My American ancestors had the neoclassical mirror made in London in the 1880s by using drawings of Robert Adam's designs. Since I come from a long line of fakers, I decided to fake the cabinet underneath it as well. London architect Christopher Smallwood drew it for me, incorporating decorative motifs from the mirror. Both are nestled in a niche with a Soanian arch.

The buffet is used for storage (overleaf). A series of drawers in the top frieze of the mahogany cabinet hold napkin rings, place cards, sets of chopsticks, and two hidden touch-latch drawers for jewelry. The bottom cabinets are reserved for tablecloths, place mats, and napkins.

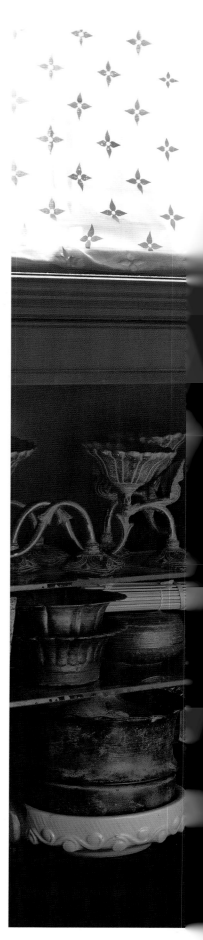

One day I was figuring out how to conjure up more storage for my ever-expanding collection of tableware, and my eyes alit upon the radiator under the dining room window. The apartment is overheated. I reasoned that I never turn the confounded thing on. So out it went. I had a cabinet retrofitted with a drop-down grille behind which I now use to stash candlesticks, vases, and other table accessories. The radiator has touch-latch cabinets behind the curtain to store wine coasters, salts and peppers, and table accessories.

THE PASS-THROUGH

There is a trend to put pass-through windows in kitchens to make serving easier. People have strong opinions about them; they either love or hate them. My client is in the former camp. The apartment is a New York pied-à-terre where she comes with children and grandchildren in tow, so ease and convenience were her top priorities. But while she asked for a pass-through window, she also wanted the choice to close it off completely to create an atmospheric dining room. When the built-in shade is lowered, the focus is on her collection of colorful hand-blown glass from Vetro Vero in Pennsylvania rather than the kitchen.

We complimented the brilliant colors of the glass by lacquering the walls in fourteen layers of copper Hollandlac paint from Fine Paints of Europe. Highlighting my client's love of lively hues, we used a silk fabric with vivid orange and green stripes for the curtains and trimmed the golden chairs with bright orange gimp. The result is cheerful and harmonious.

Since the dining room measures 11 by 12 feet, an expandable table had to be custom-made to fit in this small area (opposite). I copied a French 1930s table base and paired it with an expandable oak tabletop that seats anywhere from four to six people. Armchairs can be cumbersome in a small space unless the arms fit under the table. Here, I customized art deco round-back chairs so they are deep yet narrow. Changing the pitch of the chairs made them more comfortable because you sink back into them.

In addition to the dining table, I had enough space to create two miniscule console tables (right). Inspired by the great art deco master Gilbert Poillerat, I designed a pair of demilune console tables and had La Forge Française fabricate them. Above, we hung a pair of Italian hand-painted mirrors that are elegantly casual and perfect for her "country in the city" taste.

In the center of the wall separating the dining room and kitchen, we cut the pass-through window. At the top, a pocket from which an automated shade in the same color of the wall emerges to close off the kitchen (overleaf). To the left of the pass-through is a jib door hiding glassware. A jib door is a door purposely made "invisible" by being flush with the wall and decorated with whatever occurs on the wall flanking it (usually base moldings). Below are five drawers for silverware, linens, and serving pieces

FAMILY PORTRAIT GALLERY

oday's dining room can serve as a gallery for family portraits. This elegant and highly functional dining room works that way. It is home to five rather dour-looking portraits of ancestors, but happily, three generations of a large family also hold celebrations here.

The dining room relates well to the adjoining entry gallery as it is covered in a subtly different hue of the same mustard-colored plaster finish. A huge flower-filled urn marks the dining room entrance.

The serving table, when not loaded with platters full of food, is used to display a silver tea service, crystal decanters, and miscellaneous items.

When you enter a dining room, you want to see something dramatic. Here, it's a fine Regency convex mirror with four candle arms, which reflects the entire space (left). Because of its extraordinary quality, neither the owner nor I wanted to obscure it with a chandelier. The room is lit, instead, with six double-arm sconces, which have the effect of enlarging the space. Beneath them is a 6-foot serving table flanked by two portraits of ancestors with picture lights. The eighteenth-century English mahogany dining table is expandable. When fully extended, it seats sixteen on antique chairs that we made jazzier with chartreuse-and-brown-striped fabric.

The room originally had a 10-foot radiator concealed behind a grille. We replaced it with a new, smaller radiator, which yielded 3 feet of space on either side to accommodate below-window cabinets for vases, candleholders, and table decorations (above). Outwardly, the cabinet looks as it used to: one long, continuous, harmonious piece.

In order to have plenty of surfaces from which to serve, we placed an antique bowfront buffet along the wall and hung another ancestral portrait above it (right). To the left of the buffet is a jib door, or a disguised door, made flush with the wall (above and right). The door opens to reveal a floor-to-ceiling closet— 4 feet wide, 10½ feet high, and 14 inches deep—that is completely lined with Pacific Silvercloth to protect a huge collection of silver objects, everything from silver trays to baby rattles. We stole this space from what was once a hall closet contiguous with the dining room.

BEDROOMS

[SANCTUARY]

The earliest Latin meaning of sanctuary is "a sacred or holy space." But in my secular world, it defines a place of refuge. It is the place where you get dressed and undressed, where we are at our most vulnerable. So in our bedrooms a sense of privacy is of primary importance. More than any other room in the house, it should always feel private and quiet. • Perhaps because of this, a bedroom should also express a certain softness and sensuality. Yet at the same time, you want colors and lighting that flatter each client's sensibility. Thus the predominance of pale blues and whites, sometimes greens, too. "Muted" is the buzzword for bedrooms. You don't want to look at something that's strong and stimulating. This is why a bedroom is often known as the woman's room. When you ask a man what he wants in a bedroom, the general response is, "Whatever she wants." It is like his gift to his wife. • Bedrooms should also be quiet for sleeping. Quiet colors, as I've mentioned, are important. But every element should inspire this restfulness. So this is not, in most cases, the place to hang the Francis Bacon painting of a pope next to the raw side of beef. Supple, light fabrics, dreamy linens, plush carpeting—all these soft textures become important. Everything you touch or sleep in should be comforting, serene, inviting. • The famous line from Hamlet always echoes in my mind when I design bedrooms: "to sleep, perchance to dream."

TOILE AND CHECKS

The clients wanted a king-size bed and a French Provençal ambience for their bedroom. So we mixed toile—a quintessentially French printed fabric that usually tells a pastoral story—with subtle Swedish checks and then opted for a calming caramel-and-cream color scheme with cerise accents. This color palette was inspired by their sublime Aubusson carpet, which is icy blue with various tones of caramel punched up with rose accents.

In addition, each spouse had special requests. His revolved around practical concerns: a bench to put on his shoes, a built-in pants press, and a spot where his neckties would all be visible. Her requests were more aesthetic (the French theme, the palette) and emotional (she was a dog lover and wanted dog art on the walls).

Every bedroom needs a comfortable chair with an ottoman, a good reading lamp, and a book table. The wife bought a collection of gilt-framed dog drawings in London that we displayed throughout the room.

The bed and the hangings and corona above are made of beige-on-cream linen toile (overleaf). The color scheme extends to the custom duvet, which was made with cotton checks and features a scalloped cerise chintz border. This soft palette is easy on the eyes. The only strong tone in the room is the red upholstery on the bench at the foot of the bed and the side chair by the window. We chose a bouclé and velvet fabric because it was durable enough to withstand the wear and tear from the suitcases frequently piled on top of the bench. Butter-yellow glazed walls with a combed checkerboard pattern pull the whole scheme together.

As a rule, closets in prewar New York apartments are not exceedingly large. A combination of well-organized closets and built-in cabinetry is essential. For this bedroom, we co-opted space from a hallway to create more storage (opposite). Here the 10-foot ceilings enabled us to use the less accessible height to store out-of-season clothes. The wife's 12-foot-long built-in cabinets are painted the same color as the walls so that the doors disappear. Double doors open to reveal four bays for hanging garments. Above the cabinets are lamps with shades that have diffusers on the bottom. These shed a soft glow, just enough to illuminate the clothes but not too bright. Another narrow wall accommodates shelves for her shoes (right).

The husband's walk-in closet is tailored to his specific needs: one part for shoes, another for shirts, and a third for pants and ties (overleaf). The man of the house is fastidious and very tall. We were able to build a pants press and a bench where he could sit down to put on his shoes inside his closet. What's more, the bench conveniently features storage for his shoes underneath the seat.

A ROOM WITHIN A ROOM

My clients wanted a serene oasis in Manhattan. This master bedroom in the Plaza Hotel faces the rear of the building and overlooks a placid garden with fountains, so it is very quiet. However, the proportions were challenging. The space has a high ceiling and is 23 feet long by only 13 feet wide.

The couple were adamant about wanting a king-size bed. Our challenge was how to fit in a bed that left only a few feet on either side without making it look disproportionate to the room. We chose pale aqua fabrics from Rogers and Goffigon and neutral walls. Dressing a four-poster bed requires an experienced upholsterer like Albert Menin but this bed necessitated nine workmen for the installation. The space also needed to function as a media room where the couple could watch television with three young children. My response was, "No problem."

The clients craved a four-poster bed. Normally, you don't make king-size beds with posters because they look too boxy. However, since the room had inordinately high ceilings, we were able to run the posts up to 10 feet to balance the mattress proportions. Building such a large bed was a technical feat. We had to get the measurements exactly right and then construct the bed in situ with a team of craftsmen, movers, and upholsterers. The bed almost became a "room within a room." We were left with just enough space for two custom mirrored nightstands.

The tester is a traditional sunburst of gathered silk with a rosette (right). Being in this bed is like looking up at a luminous blue sky.

In order to create a media space, a television was mounted on the wall above the desk. At the foot of the bed, we placed a love seat and one of my favorite finds: a three-part coffee table that expands so that it can be laden with popcorn and other snacks on movie night. The rest of the time, the two smaller tables nest underneath the larger unit. The kids have their own pull-up chairs, which they picked out especially for this room.

I found a lovely painting of a woman looking out of a window by the late-nineteenth-century French artist Charles Camarroque at W. M. Brady & Company in New York (left and overleaf). It becomes the focal point when entering the bedroom from a long hallway and expands the space by making the visitor feel as if he or she were also looking out a window. A comfy reading chair with an ottoman and one of the girls' chairs were placed beneath it, creating a conversation area—"a room within a room." To the right of the bed is a small Bill Jacklin painting of a snow scene in Central Park. Purchased from Marlborough Gallery, the painting echoes the color scheme of the linens, which are from Casa del Bianco.

MASTER CLASS IN
MASTER BEDROOMS

I was traveling in Uzbekistan when I received an urgent text message informing me that my upstairs neighbor's radiator had been leaking, undetected, into my bedroom wall for weeks. I read on: "We've discovered 6-inch bands of mold around all your curtains. What should we do?" I kicked off my *makhsis* (my pointy-toed Uzbecki slippers) in a rage, screamed bloody murder, and composed a simple response: "Mold spreads. Get them out of there in the next ten minutes!" To add insult to injury, a week later when I'd arrived home to survey the damage, I promptly caught my Manolo Blahniks on a sisal carpet and careened into a doorframe, breaking my shoulder and back. So there I was, with a moldy bedroom that had no curtains and that had to be gutted and redone—and injuries that left me barely mobile. The doctors told me not to go to the D&D building because of its crowded elevators.

As sitting still has never been my forte, on the way home from the doctor's one day, I happened to walk by Baranzelli, a discount fabric store on Third Avenue. I loathed my ugly institutional sling and decided to make my own with a bit of velvet and some tassels, ever the chic decorator. As I poked around the bolts, my thoughts turned to my ruined bedroom and something dawned on me: why not buy all the fabrics right then and there? In 10 minutes, I picked out a bolt of off-white cotton linen for the new curtains. In addition, I bought 30 yards of blue cotton linen for the bed, chair, and ottoman; 8 yards of silk velvet for two slipper chairs; 4 yards of a printed linen for a table skirt; and Ultrasuede in two colors simply because I liked both shades. Then I took a taxi to M&J Trimming on Sixth Avenue and bought coarse, undyed trims and miles of hemp and jute cording to finish the edges of my bed and reading chair. I wanted the trims to look natural.

I get great pleasure from the beautiful bed and silk velvet chairs. But the real beauty is the room's practicality. To the right of the bed are 14 linear feet of closets behind millwork. People who come into the room don't know I'm sleeping on five sets of suitcases and six sets of bed linens located in modular boxes under my bed. All they see is a luxurious bedroom. They have no idea how functional and easy this space is to live in.

The bed is a reproduction of one found at Mallett Antiques in London. I assembled it with the help of the baronet and eminent antiquarian Sir Humphry Wakefield. At the foot of the bed, two Victorian chairs purchased years ago in London and re-covered in silk velvet add texture. The fresh color palette and an absence of fussy pattern make for a more modern, down-to-earth sensibility.

The bedside lamps are made from Indonesian fish traps. Rather than pleated silk, I used paper drum shades, which give them a more casual look. Other contemporizing tricks include storing my countless silver picture frames in the basement because I'm not polishing them any more; changing all the decorative hardware from showy brass to more subdued nickel and glass; and reframing my botanical prints by Roy McCune, a rock star and artist from the 1960s, with simple wood and plain mats. The floor is covered with a subtle beige pattern. My former glazed walls are now painted in Farrow & Ball paint—two flat coats cover the old glossy glaze.

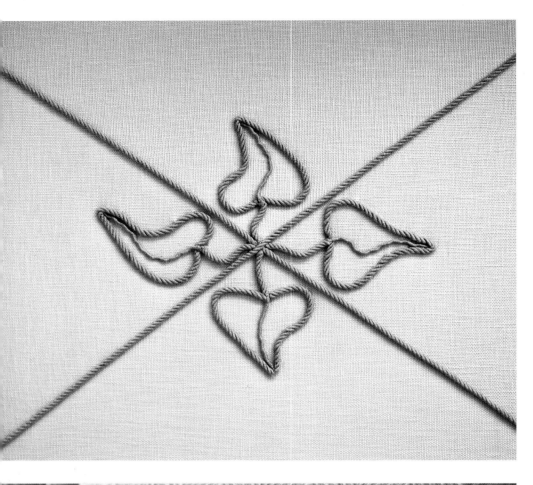

At Baranzelli, I had another epiphany. What I really wanted for the headboard was "my" fantasy tree, inspired by a second century B.C. motif from Delos (opposite). The builders of the Villa Kérylos in Beaulieu-sur-mer, France, adopted the Greek motif for the dressing room—and that's where I fell in love with it. I know this tree is "fantasy" because I asked curators at the Metropolitan Museum of Art and the director of the Villa Kérylos to identify "my" tree and they all agreed: it bears no relationship to any known species. To reproduce it, we first projected an image onto a bedsheet the size of my headboard. To fill empty spots, branches and blossoms were added until the new tree fully "grew" into the given space. Penn & Fietcher embroidered "my" tree in string, hemp, and Ultrasuede on blue linen. Playing off the color scheme of the headboard, I had two sets of linens made: brown for winter, blue for summer.

For under the top of the bed canopy, a Nigerian upholsterer at Albert Menin and I created a leaf design by unwinding thick hemp rope and hand-twisting thinner strands of it into a more delicate cord to form the outlines of foliage (top left). The boudoir pillows were custom embroidered in Madagascar by Julia B. Linens (bottom left). Since I often read in this comfortable bed, I had swing-arm lamps installed in addition to the bedside table lamps. One set of lamps eliminates the shadows of the other.

I had four square modular boxes on wheels made for under the bed, two of which store my linens, the other two weekend suitcases (opposite). It was only possible to do this by raising the bed frame and using a 3-inch custom-made box spring and a thinner mattress. For the bedside tables, I repurposed an eighteenth-century American serving table and an antique French commode—both are about 34 inches high.

There is a wealth of storage in the cabinets lining the wall. Three of them open to reveal double-hung rods for suits, dresses, blouses, and jackets (top right). The rods are adjustable so that if hemlines go up or down, I can adapt to current fashion. A fourth cabinet contains drawers for gloves, scarves, and exercise clothes. The one closest to the door is set aside for my extensive shoe collection (bottom right). I created nineteen thin shelves and had them installed toward the back half of the cabinet, which now accommodate fifty-seven pairs of flat shoes. The box door, with twelve more shelves holding twenty-four more pairs of heels, fits into the front half of the cabinet when closed.

Eight feet is as high as you can usually go before a closet or cabinet door begins to warp, but I have 10-foot ceilings. Never one to waste an inch, I had cubbyholes made across the entire length above the cabinets. These contain out-of-season pocketbooks, summer hats, and safari and Western wear.

The envy of every woman who comes into this room are the five sideways jewelry drawers that are squeezed into a corner of the room. When the drawers are closed, all you see in that corner is an Italianate gilded chair covered in Ultrasuede. But pull the knob on the wall next to it and you'll find a drawer that slides out to reveal racks for earrings or necklaces. At the opposite end of that wall of cabinetry are two hooks for hanging clothes that have returned from the dry cleaner or must be ironed (opposite). Every bedroom needs a few hooks like these.

Opposite the bed is a skirted table covered in a Greek patterned cotton. It used to hold a television, but who's got time to watch TV these days? Now, one side of it disguises motorized file cabinets that lift up at the touch of a button (above). The other side has drawers with exercise weights, a yoga mat, and anything else for a home gym (overleaf). Drawers above this function as a stash for jewelry boxes, travel cases, lost keys, and other odds and ends.

On the top surface I've assembled vanity trays from Greece, Peru, England, and other locales. I deposit my jewelry there until I can put it away.

To the left of the skirted table is a closet for sweaters, which I outfitted with fifteen thin shelves on gliders (above). At the back of each is a Plexiglas barrier that keeps sweaters from falling behind the shelves. The transparency of the Plexiglas also means that you can see down to the next shelf. It's particularly useful for those black turtlenecks. Most women have many, and they can never seem to find *the one* they're looking for.

In the corner, to the right of the skirted table, is a closet where I hang evening gowns (opposite). One of the doors is a dummy, put there to balance the other side, where double doors conceal the sweater shelves. I don't have to get in there every day, so it is the perfect place for a large armchair and ottoman, where I can sit and read.

OOO LA LA LOLLIPOP

I t's wonderful to work with a client who is experimental and loves brilliant colors. Color serves many functions, from helping segregate a space within a space to making you just plain happy, or calm or stimulated. And when it comes to children, it's absolutely essential. How many kids do you know who crave an all-white or ecru bedroom? Left to their own devices, children would paint their walls lilac, bubble gum pink, red, or royal blue. You can be adventurous with kids' rooms, though you also have to strike a balance. The client in this case had a pretty intrepid attitude toward color and wanted her little girls, who share this room, to have a space that was fun and bright. So we just spun the liveliest section of the color wheel and away we went.

Enough color, you ask? You must be joking. How could we deliver delight if we didn't push the envelope? We designed four Ultrasuede lollipop chairs in fuchsia, deep turquoise, bold tangerine, and royal blue, with contrasting leather welts, and gathered them around a small table that we had made for the tight space (opposite). With all that color, we did have the sense to realize that if we filled the room with a lot of pattern, it would look like a bad hallucinogenic 1960s pad. So we included only two subtle patterns: a soft green plaid for the wall-to-wall carpet and stripes of mauve, mint, and white for the curtains.

Naturally, the place provides maximum storage. The closet has adjustable triple-hung racks for clothes and linens and oodles of shelves for everything else. We also gave the girls a freestanding open cabinet from Pottery Barn and stocked it with baskets for their toys (right).

Since this is a pied-à-terre and not a full-time house, the room had to serve many needs. It would be a bedroom, a playroom, and a place to do homework and projects. The two multipurpose box tables are made of a pliable material so they can be easily folded and stashed in the closet. We swapped the colors, putting the fuchsia lid on the cantaloupe box, and the cantaloupe on the fuchsia box. These inexpensive boxes not only hold toys but you can also sit on them. Blue and pink throws, as well as paper lampshades in various saturated tones, add more pops of color.

Walking by Barneys New York one day, I spotted a street artist named Peter Zonis, who creates colorful paintings of Manhattan, and commissioned him to do three fun views of New York. I put his painting of the Plaza Hotel, particularly appropriate because this apartment is in that historic building, over the mauve sofa.

No one loves sleepovers more than little girls, so this room had to sleep at least four comfortably. We started with two trundle beds, one in mauve with green pillows, the other in green with mauve pillows (overleaf). When the trundles are pulled out, the room becomes one vast platform. Casa del Bianco embroidered the linens, incorporating various tones from the room into the borders. Notice that the two anchoring colors, fuchsia and acid green, are saturated without being loud. That freed us up to use deeper shades as accents.

MEN'S
DRESSING ROOMS

[EFFICIENCY]

Every man wants a dressing room of his own, where he can get up early in the morning, dress, and pack without disturbing anyone. The main thing I've learned about designing them over the years is this: men are predictable. Yet there is great pleasure for a designer in that kind of regularity. Women's wardrobes are in a state of perpetual evolution. Men don't have to deal with fluctuating hemlines. And with men, you know if they fold their shirts or hang them. You know their shoes are all going to be flat-heeled. You know whether they hang their pants short or long.   •   The other thing I've learned is that men tend to know *exactly* what they want. You can ask them what kind of style they'd like for a living room and most will say, "Oh, I don't care." But when it comes to their dressing room, they're meticulous about keeping sports equipment here, country clothes there. They want specific compartments for gloves, cuff links, and watches. They want a place to sit to put on their socks and shoes. Men's dressing rooms are completely about practicality. By measuring shirts and under-wear, customized compartmentalized drawers can be built for a man's every need.

HERMÈS IN PARIS

ermès style is legendary. So when you design a dressing room for someone like Xavier Guerrand-Hermès, one of the directors of the Paris fashion and luxury goods house, you need the highest quality design and execution. But it should also serve the needs of a man who is both acquisitive and peripatetic.

Basic closet systems, even beautiful high-end ones, didn't have enough character for Xavier, who wanted something that reflected his deep appreciation of North African culture. Working with him to channel his exotic sense of style into a functional space that fit his needs like an immaculately tailored suit was one of the most enjoyable experiences of my career. He was my first client, and he became my favorite repeat client.

Filling the whole space with floor-to-ceiling cabinets would have felt claustrophobic, so we took another tack, incorporating art and furniture. Since we were basing the whole design on Arab themes, a Damascene dresser with intricate mother-of-pearl inlay was a natural choice (and much more interesting than a modular unit that matched the millwork surrounding it). Above it he placed an Orientalist painting and various figurines of Arabs (two of them on carved brackets). The art and accessories distract from the purely functional closets and make the room seem like an exotic kasbah. It's a fantastic room.

Xavier came up with the clever idea of substituting the typical solid doors of closets with customized screened doors made with spear-like dowels and backed with pale silks. They provide another layer of personalization and make the space feel airier than one with solid cabinetry. Above each door is a brass rail on which a movable ladder can be hooked to access the upper cabinets.

As Xavier travels a great deal, he needed easy access to storage for packing. So we placed a tall, custom packing table in the center of the room, where he can lay a suitcase. The drawers below this table hold undergarments and other practical things you'd throw in a suitcase. All the cabinetry is light colored because it helps counter the darkness of the room. One compartment contains orange boxes: Hermès items for hostess gifts.

The overall effect of Xavier's dressing room resembles a chic haberdashery. The interiors of the closets are organized for a substantial wardrobe, accommodating suits on double-hung rods, luggage, and shoes. A separate closet has pullout shelves for shirts and a pullout tie rack. I could swear Xavier owns one of every Hermès tie pattern ever conceived. Two hanging mirrors flank the dresser, making it easier to see and brightening the space with dancing light. By the carved mirror, we created a storage area for large suitcases hidden behind silk panels (opposite).

A MAN'S OWN BESPOKE RETREAT

The most important aspect of dressing rooms is cabinets. They are far more space efficient than a walk-in closet, as space is not lost to hallways. This was not your average dressing room. The client, an entrepreneur with a large, elegant wardrobe, wanted a space that functioned as a dressing room, a private retreat to make business calls, and an oasis to which he could retire with a book. That's a tall order for just 300 square feet. It required meticulous analysis of every item of apparel so that we could stash everything out of sight and make the room look like a manly and comfortable library. With its hand-blocked wallpaper from Christopher Hyland, a handsome new fireplace mantel, and a grouping of antiques, you wouldn't know this is a dressing room unless you started opening cabinets. The painted cabinets with raised panels cover an entire wall.

The low console, purchased from a private London dealer, conceals the client's television (right). Atop is a gallery of family photographs and boxes for cuff links and watches. Black lamps with custom overscaled lampshades and bronze decorations boast masculine silhouettes. They flank a gilded mirror, also custom-made to fit the space.

One wall of this dressing room is devoted to cabinets. We measured all his folded shirts and designed Plexiglas-fronted drawers for them so he could effortlessly find what he was looking for.

The interior of each drawer is measured specficially for its contents: shirts, socks, shoes, and freshly laundered folded shirts (opposite). This kind of organizational system helps him quickly choose his clothes.

    We also measured his suits and jackets and, after telling him to get rid of a few, hung them on double racks. The German-made Häfele hardware they hang from is adjustable, just in case men's jacket lengths get longer. The tie racks, frankly, are a bit of genius (above). Most often, tie racks are made of metal or wood and ties are constantly sliding off them and onto the floor. My solution was to cover the rods with suede, then finish the ends with attractive brass finials.

The elaborately carved mantel provides the visual focus for the room, which consists of mostly Regency-era furnishings. The suede-covered, wood-frame armchair is from a private London dealer. The chest-on-chest, atop which we stacked suitcases for our peripatetic client, came from Florian Papp. It's an elegant piece of furniture that also multiplies the storage capacity of the room. Florian Papp was also the source of the lamps in the room. A table that looks like stacked books emphasizes the library idea and provides a surface for a lamp to read by in the comfortably upholstered armchair and ottoman.

SMALL KITCHENS

[ECONOMY OF SPACE]

Designing a small kitchen is a challenge. There are many practical demands for such a compact space. It has to be logically planned. Where people stand to cook and clean, how drawers and large appliances open, which amenities fit, and which ones the client must sacrifice due to space constraints—every minute detail must be carefully considered. • Nevertheless, as challenging as they are, I love working on small kitchens. It's similar to designing a kitchen for a boat or an airplane. In fact, I draw on many of the technologies and techniques regularly employed in these modes of transport. Mechanized lifts that reveal or conceal small appliances, for instance, were developed for boats and planes, but they are lifesavers in the tight space of a typical New York City kitchen. Using thinner materials—such as slimmer marble (there's another ¾ inch)—creates a surprising amount of room. • Designing small kitchens requires a talented carpenter patient enough to understand that every ⅛ of an inch matters. You can use tricks to visually expand the space, such as undercounter lighting and a mirror for the backsplash. But in the end, you're still working with a finite amount of inches and feet. • Wood is the softest surface underfoot, and since my floor is only 3 feet by 4 feet, it seems to beg for one with "historical" markings. I thought of initializing it, but one of my cousins said, "It's time to send out for the family crest." So I did. A Russian marquetry artist fashioned the cartouche and shield in fourteen rare woods. Such an unusual yet personal touch often stops traffic. Who else is going to put their family crest on the floor?

HERMÈS
MOROCCAN GALLEY

Years ago I unexpectedly ran into Xavier Guerrand-Hermès at a phone booth on Lexington Avenue. We were by then longtime friends and had both just returned from living in Indonesia. He wanted my help in realizing an unusual idea he had envisioned for his New York apartment: an entry upholstered in Indonesian batik with orange baseboards and a brown bedroom upholstered with an Hermès print of Islamic warriors riding to battle.

Several years later, he wanted to collaborate on his kitchen, which he was completely gutting. But if I thought this would be any calmer than our first adventure, I was dead wrong. He asked for a Moroccan-inspired kitchen, something that reminded him of the place where he spends much of his time. The French have all sorts of special requests, and Xavier was no exception. He would require extensive storage for wine, dishes, and entertaining supplies.

That was fine, except this was a galley kitchen just 20 feet long by 8 feet wide—a mere 160 square feet. My organizational mind kicked into high gear, and I set to work. Xavier is a consummate host, which means the apartment was the setting for frequent dinner parties, great and small. And he is an intuitive cook—a pinch of this, a dab of that—so he needs a space where he can let his creative culinary mind roam without people underfoot. Yet he still needs to interact with friends while cooking.

My solution was to divide the kitchen into two areas: a butler's pantry and bar, and a cooking area with a counter by the window that could serve as both breakfast nook and home office. The design process was like building a boat. Every piece was outfitted to within a ¼ inch of its life.

Green is the color of Islam, so why not use it to drive the palette for a Moroccan kitchen? Just as a green oasis means water in a desert, green in the Qur'an represents paradise. The warmly toned natural wood frames of the cabinets are inset either with raised, green-stained wood panels or textured green-colored glass. Green granite countertops add even more texture. Everything Xavier might need is located within arm's reach in the area near the window: pots hanging from a custom rack suspended from the ceiling; dishes behind the green-glass overhead cabinets; a sink and counter space on one side; a range, refrigerator; and more counter space opposite. We then raised the counters 2 inches above the standard 36 inches so Xavier would not have to strain his back by bending over cutting boards and mixing bowls.

All the drawers and cabinets by the stove top are designed to keep frequently used ingredients within easy reach, as well as to store serving pieces. In New York apartments, who has space to waste with an inert toe kick? We used this space to house touch-latch drawers that pull out for added storage. The terra-cotta-and-green tile floor is pure Moroccan in inspiration.

Opposite the kitchen window we installed a wet bar by robbing space—like two of Ali Baba's enterprising thieves—from another kitchen entry (opposite). The bar has storage above and below and also provides a second food prep area, which makes it possible for two people to work simultaneously. Someone can fix drinks and hors d'oeuvres and still manage to stay out of the way of the principal cook. To the right of the refrigerator, under another small countertop, is a wine cooler that stores up to 160 bottles of wine. *Vive la France*! And that 18-inch-wide floor-to-ceiling cabinet by the service entrance? This shallow pantry hides an unsightly electrical panel.

What a nicely finished corner by the wet bar, you might say (above). Well, it's not there just for looks. Pull on the little knob and you'll discover a hinged door that conceals a trim but highly useful closet for a vacuum cleaner, ironing board, broom, and cleaning supplies.

STEPHANIE'S JEWEL BOX

Caterers tell me it's easier to work in my compact kitchen than in many sprawling, glamorous ones. How's that for a compliment. My kitchen is logical. When you open a cabinet, you find what you're expecting to find, and you're never more than one step from anything you need. There is no reason to travel vast distances just to bring a mixing bowl to the counter where you're working.

When I designed it, the plan for the kitchen was limited by the New York City laws of the time, which stipulated that if a kitchen didn't have a window, it could not be larger than 48 square feet. Mine does not have a window and is exactly 7 feet by 7 feet, so it was important to think through all my needs. It helped that I could store all my glasses above the wet bar in the library and install a refrigerator in what was legally "the butler's pantry." Specifically, this meant I could utilize my very limited space in the kitchen for my vast collection of china. And because the bar in the library has a small dishwasher, all good crystal and glass are washed there, leaving my kitchen countertops empty when entertaining. The 10-foot-high ceilings meant I could expand storage upward and access it with a ladder. Unlike most kitchens, the china shelves are not evenly spaced. That's because I sacrificed perfect symmetry for function, designing the shelves to accommodate the china I had, rather than trying to fit the china inefficiently into standard-issue shelving. The shelves are also thinner than usual so I can fit as much as possible into them. My kitchen is a gem. And it was given the "Kitchen of the Month" award by *House Beautiful* in July 2008.

With so little space, I wanted simple white cabinetry modeled on Shaker prototypes. Since the kitchen is windowless (opposite), I used a green marble countertop, which brings in colors from nature. The bottom of the overhead cabinets is also lower than normal, which means the backsplash is 18 inches high instead of 22 inches. I did this to maximize storage (it gave me 4 extra inches all around for more china). This also makes it easier to retrieve plates from the lower shelves. A 5-foot, 5-inch woman would rather reach things easily than have headroom. To keep it all from getting too claustrophobic, I mirrored the backsplashes and installed incandescent undercounter lighting throughout, instantly expanding the space visually, if not physically.

In the wall separating the kitchen from the entry hall, I used a 4-inch recess between two studs to house a stepladder (above) so I could reach all the higher shelves in the kitchen and store bottles of water. The ladder is not hung; it is held in place with a magnet.

Above the electric range is a shelf that is particularly shallow (the exhaust is just behind it). That's where I put a stainless-steel Rösle hanging system for often-used utensils, salt and pepper, and a clock (right). This organizational system makes a space that is less than 3 inches deep into a highly functioning storage unit. The cabinet above is built around the same ductwork and stores china. Here, as in other cabinetry, I used thinner than normal shelves because I had to house fourteen sets of dishes collected from my travels. On either side of the center cabinet are pullout pantries (above).

Three drawers are lined with antitarnish Pacific Silvercloth to house my silver. Open cabinets below the cooktop are home to cookbooks, baking sheets, and cutting boards. Even the toe kick is utilized. All you need are 4 inches to install long, flat drawers, also lined with Pacific Silvercloth, for silver serving trays (page 158). Drawers above them accommodate spices (alphabetized, naturally), teas, cooking utensils, hot pads, and other necessities. One drawer is reserved for glass bowls and measuring cups. Below a deep recycling drawer is a second deep space for tea and coffee pots.

Perpendicular to the center cabinet are glass-fronted ones for still more dishes. That's surely the most I could wring from overhead dish storage, you might say. Au contraire. I adopted a motorized technology often used on boats and planes, creating two appliance garages that drop down from the corners closest to the backsplash, which are inaccessible spaces in most kitchens (above). Hit a switch and down comes the Cuisinart or the toaster. My knives slip right into the kitchen counter, eliminating the need for a big wood knife block that takes up so much space.

DINE · DEN LIVE · KITCH

[THE HUB OF THE HOUSE]

A "dine-den-live-kitch" is essentially the physical manifestation of the way most Americans live today. They no longer simply cook in the kitchen. They eat, serve drinks, entertain, feed the pets, lounge, listen to music, and talk on the phone. They make it into an indestructible family room where the children watch television, play, and do homework. The head of the household manages the house from a desk in the kitchen. There is often a bar, an island where guests can help or chat with the cook, an area for the dog with all its attendant accoutrements (leashes, treats, bowls, and toys), and, of course, a place for audio and visual equipment: computers, iPads, iPods, chargers, wall-mounted landline phones, and so on.   •   These changes in lifestyle drive design today. As Americans become more casual, designers must facilitate their new needs, which requires a great deal of forethought. Contemporary kitchens have multiple functions. They should be equipped with up-to-date appliances in addition to being comfortable spaces. There needs to be ample storage for not only kitchen equipment and utensils but also technology, paperwork, pets, and much more.

GOURMET COOKING WITH GRANDCHILDREN

This kind of kitchen is my most typical New York job. It involves taking an old-fashioned design and reimagining it for the contemporary user to actually use. Prewar apartments were commonly constructed with quarters for a live-in staff, and in those days, the kitchen was off limits to everyone else. Most people don't live that way anymore. Today the kitchen is the centerpiece of family life.

My clients bought the apartment in the 1970s and raised their family in it. When I came on the job, their children had married and were out of the house, so the couple's needs had changed. The wife is a superb cook and required more space in which to create her exceptional meals. So we gutted what had been two maids' rooms, a bath, a servants' dining room, a laundry room, and a butler's pantry, replacing it with what I call a "dine-den-live-kitch" (dining and living areas and a kitchen, all open to one another). An exercise room, bathroom, and new laundry room are located nearby.

We designed the space by going through my clients' old kitchen and analyzing what was important to their lifestyle. They are inveterate and tireless entertainers. Grandchildren were an important consideration, too, so childproofing features needed to be incorporated. Our main coup was creating a floor plan that gives the impression of entering a family room, not a kitchen. The first thing you see is a cozy banquette. This has become Grand Central Station for the grandchildren. We asked a fabric supplier, "What's the toughest thing you have that we could drive trucks over and not ruin?" The answer was a tough, woven multicolored bouclé, a fabric that can take a beating. Its lively pattern also performs wonders for hiding spills. The simple ladder-back chairs and farm table are durable, too.

This extraordinary dine-den-live-kitch is both practical and efficient. It is divided into four zones—cook, eat, work, drink. Every essential accessory for the serious cook has been taken into account: a Wolf range, double ovens, and even a warming drawer, which opens out from under a long, polished stone-topped counter (opposite). Common in England, this useful piece of equipment is rarely part of the American kitchen.

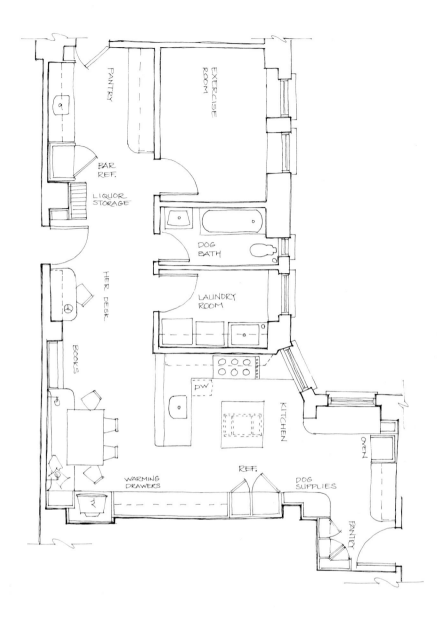

The plan shows the many functions of this dine-den-live-kitch, from a bar area for entertaining to a workstation for running the household (above). This part of the prewar apartment was also reconfigured to include a laundry room, where one can iron in privacy, a home gym, and even a bath to pamper their pooch. One important request was for a dining niche opposite the cooking area (left). This way, the kitchen island creates two distinct spaces—one for the cook and one for guests and grandchildren to gather.

The wife required a command center from which to run the home (right). Her command center has everything she needs to manage the household: a bulletin board crisscrossed with ribbon for posting notes and to-do lists, drawers for desk supplies, and overhead cabinetry. Between the desk and the banquette are built-in shelves that accommodate file cabinets, cookbooks, a fax machine and printer, and more. Built-ins on the opposite side store additional cookbooks and the television.

I'm not a fan of the de rigueur 1½ inch-thick marble countertops. The countertops here are just ¾ inch thick. They're more tasteful and have the added advantage of affording extra space for cabinetry below. Pots are easily accessible from a rack overhead (opposite).

Next to the dining niche are drawers for linens and cabinets for coffee cups and mugs. The proximity of these storage units makes it easy to set the table and to grab a cup for coffee without bothering the cook (right, top and bottom).

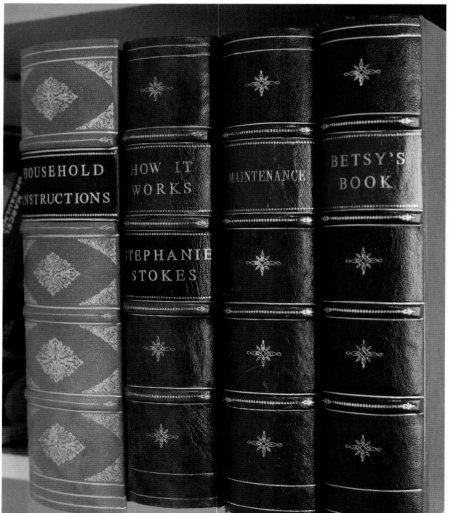

This is the husband's corner. He asked for extra storage for wine and spirits, and we delivered. Fifteen open wine storage bins can hold up to ten cases (opposite). Below these, four deep drawers pull out to reveal a prodigious stock of liquor (above). Around the corner are shelves for mixers.

On one of the shelves by the storage for wine and spirits, we placed several leather-bound volumes that were custom-made in London for our client (left). Their contents relate to various aspects of home management, including warranty and maintenance information for every appliance, telephone numbers, instruction manuals, menus, and more. We always give clients a set of such handy organizers as a courtesy.

A butler's pantry connects the "dine-den-live-kitch" with the formal dining room (opposite). One end of the counter has open shelves for displaying the clients' collections of transferware. Overhead cabinetry accommodates no fewer than 120 pieces of glassware for cocktail parties—from tumblers and highballs to goblets to Pottery Barn glasses. Wood floors stained a traditional warm brown continue the aesthetic of the rest of the apartment, unifying the design. This area allows residents and visitors to make their own drinks or pour themselves a cup of coffee without intruding on the busy cooking area. The butler's pantry also serves as storage for formal silver housed in drawers lined with Pacific Silvercloth and linens of every variety (right, top and bottom).

Convenient pullout shelves house mixing bowls and cookware (page 186, top). Slots in the granite counters enable easy, accessible storage for knives (page 186, bottom). They also keep sharp blades out of children's reach. Thin, painted Masonite panels can be adjusted thanks to grooved wood on the top and bottom of the cabinet, allowing the hostess to customize her storage. Keeping trays and serving pieces vertical also saves space (page 187).

Another cabinet opens to reveal shelves devoted to dog treats, food, bowls, leashes, and other canine paraphernalia (left).

By the door to the service elevator, there is a space just 4½ inches deep (opposite). Most people would hang a picture and call it a day. We utilized this shallow area for pantry storage. Since the shelves aren't deep, there's no chance of losing your Tabasco behind the soy sauce. Everything in the cabinet is fully visible.

FRENCH TWIST

This Westchester client was a big fan of French country style. So what better place to go for a Provençal kitchen than Howard Kaplan Designs? This is my ode to Howard, the man who pioneered the style in the United States. Chairs, table, accessories, almost everything came from his charming emporium in lower Manhattan. When it came to "smalls" (what designers call the knickknacks that fill out a room and give it personality), we just went to Howard's and loaded a truck.

But lest you think it's all aesthetics, let me assure you that the kitchen/family room is jam-packed with function. There were several demands, each calling for its own "zone." Not only is the client a major cook, but, having been a powerful businesswoman before taking a break to raise her family, she also wanted an office area to run her busy life and a workstation for her kids to do homework together. She also asked for a sitting area for watching television and gathering with the children. The back door opens into the kitchen from the garage, so a "mudroom" was necessary. We were able to deliver all the zones.

The color palette is pure French, derived from a standard Provençal fabric with a green and orangey-red floral plaid pattern woven into the yellow ground. You see this kind of woven pattern on tablecloths throughout Provence.

The dining space of the "dine-den-live-kitch" is sundrenched. The various rugs in this hub help delineate the eating and sitting areas. Here, we bound two pieces of carpet in the bright colors of the curtains and pillows. The round breakfast table encourages conversation and interaction and is surrounded by wheat-back chairs, typical of French country style. The setting is crowned with a Dutch blue-and-white porcelain chandelier from Manhattan antiques dealer David Duncan. We built a rack under one of the large windows to keep newspapers and magazines accessible but orderly.

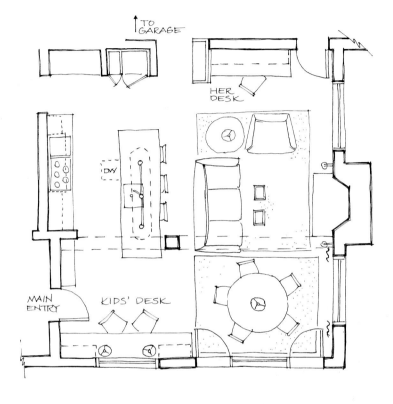

For the "dine-den-live-kitch," a large kitchen island separates the family room from the cooking space (see floor plan above and left). We created a timeless look by installing a white kitchen with black granite countertops. A carrot looks better on black granite, and a tomato looks even better—it enhances the color of the fresh foods you're preparing. Pulled up to the island are stools with the same wheat motif as the chairs around the breakfast table. Overhead is an enormous pot rack from Howard Kaplan Designs with three light fixtures. The fabrics had to be durable but comfortable, so we used chenille on the sofa in the sitting area. The pillows, made with a square-within-a-square pattern and featuring mitered corners, are cotton with fuzzy, woolly edges. They're a joy to see and soft to touch.

The kneehole of the children's desk is wide enough for two, so a parent can help a child with homework, or the kids can play computer games simultaneously (left). There are plenty of drawers for school supplies and shelves above. To avoid scratching the wood floors, my client cut tennis balls and slipped them over the ends of the chair legs. It's hysterical looking, but it works.

She loves roosters (how French!) so we created shelves at one end of the island to accommodate a barnyard full of roosters (opposite). A wooden wine rack down the middle holds a dozen bottles, and around the corner, against the stove wall, is a second cooler for more wine and champagne.

The client's "command center" is opposite the kids' workstation (above). The interior of her built-in desk was custom-designed to accommodate a printer and reams of paper, both of which are easily accessed on pullout shelves. The other side holds massive file cabinets. We also gave her a custom bulletin board, dressing it up with red ribbon on green felt.

Around the corner is an area that does double duty as "mudroom" and storage for dog paraphernalia (opposite). Leashes, treats, and doggie toys hang on hooks and fit into cubbies in the top half of the storage unit. A shelf at bench height serves as a perch for removing boots, which, once removed, are then neatly stored on a lower shelf. The back entry is tiled to make it easy to clean, which is important, since the family, like many, uses this entrance rather than the front door.

ENTRIES AND MUDROOMS

[FIRST IMPRESSION]

Entries are essentially "trailers"—snippets of what is to come. When you step inside a house, you should immediately know what to expect. Is it going to be grand or casual, family-oriented or elegant, whimsical or erudite? You want an entry to convey the mood. When entering, you know if the house is comfortable, intimate, aesthetically pleasing, or any combination thereof.   •   All entries, whether on a Colorado ranch or in a Park Avenue apartment, have similar practical concerns: a place to drop packages and keys, to hang up a coat, and to remove boots. Women want a mirror to check their appearance. Entries should be comparatively void of furniture because guests accumulate there. On the other hand, entries, like powder rooms, are opportunities to let your imagination run wild. The possibilities for decorating are limitless.

ANGLO-INDIAN BARN

This Sagaponack, Long Island, project is really two projects. The clients had a barn they converted into a living space. An addition was built—the main entry connects the old barn with the new structure, which is composed of several bedrooms off a single long hallway. One side of that hallway has French doors that open onto the pool area so guests can access rooms without entering the main house. Our challenge was to connect the old and new elements in a way that appeared seamless.

The husband loves Anglo-Indian furniture. To shake things up a bit (and to avoid a one-note interior), I expanded this collecting passion beyond its strict definition, which would have limited our choices to furnishings of the British Raj style. Instead, I drew from a larger sweep of the Empire, including furniture from French Caribbean holdings as well as from America (whose colonial styles were largely influenced by English design trends of the seventeenth and eighteenth centuries). I peppered this design scheme with other pieces within the vocabulary of the Indian subcontinent's colonial aesthetic: furnishings from Goa, the former Portuguese colony that is now part of India.

In the main entry that connects the barn to the addition, we centered the decor around a French Caribbean table, which sits atop a sisal rug bound in deep red leather (opposite). A forged French pendant used as a chandelier hangs above this table, where guests can always find the latest books to read. Reproduction Anglo-Indian dining chairs from British Khaki flank a cabinet from Barbados that was purchased from Michael Connors, a dealer who specializes in Caribbean furniture.

The clients needed a closet for coats, boots, tack, and hats in the entry but did not want clutter, so we concealed the closet behind the wall with the settee and papered it in a very French way with purple and green stripes (right). After all, why should closets be plain and uninteresting? The pew on the left was salvaged from an old Caribbean church. We placed it in the hallway en route to the walk-in closet.

The round center table from Martinique serves as a drop for piles of illustrated books. An overscaled brown vase holds huge welcoming bouquets. Against the wall is a cane settee from Goa. We upholstered the cushion in cotton Madras plaid and gave it a "mattress" detail. Above it is a mirror from British Khaki.

A long hallway runs from the new entry to a covered patio, where we placed two chaises that Bali-based designer Linda Garland originally made for David Bowie (opposite and above). The French doors to the right side of the hallway open onto the pool. Along the left side are more doors that lead into three bedrooms and a courtyard. The floor is made of reclaimed pine from North Carolina barns, which connects it visually to the original building. To break up the potential tunnel effect of such a long and narrow space, we scattered Oriental rugs and divided the hall into sections: a colonial American serving table anchors the middle of the hall. An upholstered bench sits close to the patio. The bell jar lanterns that line the hallway are from India.

SHOWCASE FOR ASIAN ART

An entry should always say something about the owner of the house. There was no doubt, when you entered this Central Park West apartment in New York City, that the client, John Gruber, was a serious collector of Asian art. So our primary concern was to create a showcase for the art. But we had additional programmatic requirements. The entry hall, which we created by annexing an adjacent doctor's office, had to double as a dining area. It was long and narrow, so we had to devise a way to mitigate the tunnel feeling. In the end, John and I agreed that we achieved what we were aiming for: namely, *shibui*, the Japanese word for understated elegance, which is the highest aesthetic goal in Japanese culture.

Mirroring the left wall instantly deepened a space that would have otherwise felt compressed. We covered the other walls with grass cloth, an extremely durable material with a warm, natural character that served as a neutral yet textured foil for the art. The floors throughout were all white ash—again, a quiet material that would not compete with the art, a perfect background for the client's antique Tibetan rugs. To provide a dining table, we bought an eighteenth-century Irish drop-leaf wake table. With its leaves down, it serves as a console; with leaves up, pulled into the center of the room, it seats twelve comfortably. It works aesthetically because wake tables are simple designs, just like the eighteenth-century Huanghuali armchairs that flank it. Above it hangs an exquisite seventeenth-century Japanese screen. To the left is a black lacquer Japanese chest.

Viewing the entry from the living room, you see a collection of Ming porcelain on the wake table (left). A Tibetan bronze stands on top of a lacquer console cabinet. The space jags to the left before opening into the living room (overleaf). John collected Japanese tansu chests and Korean cabinets. On the right, a Korean piece is situated in the ell of the entryway, close enough to the living room to serve as a storage receptacle for linens and other table decorations. To the right of the cabinet hangs a Korean painting, and a Tibetan rug lies on the floor. Two Chinese scholars benches from the Ch'ing dynasty were placed below the painting.

At the end of the bedroom hall is an antique Chinese medicine cabinet with lots of little drawers (overleaf, top right). You'd be amazed at how useful such drawers can be for holding all manner of small items: light bulbs, batteries, screws, picture hooks—the list is endless. Near the bedroom is another important Korean chest (overleaf, bottom right). An Edo period (early to mid-nineteenth-century) lacquer lamp from the Akasen "red light" district that was wired for electricity sits to the right of the chest.

COCTEAU
AT THE PLAZA

New York City has too many overly grand entrances in my opinion. We could have opted for a formal entrance here, in the hallowed precincts of the converted Plaza Hotel—arguably the benchmark of chic in turn-of-the-twentieth-century luxury hotels—but we chose not to. Why? Because I was designing an apartment not only for adult clients but also for their three young children. And those children like to invite their friends over. While we didn't need to make the place an amusement park fun house, we also didn't feel compelled to go for all-out formality.

A console with a mirror is a completely appropriate and practical setup (opposite). It provides a place to drop your keys and gloves after entering—and a reflective surface to check your appearance, whether you are coming in or going out. While it was a no-brainer, we resisted the impulse to go with antiques as they might intimidate children. Instead, we had London furniture craftsman Thomas Messel make a bright red velvet curvaceous baroque table, accentuated with hundreds of antiqued brass studs. The mirror, a pared-down Swedish piece, gracefully fills out the incredibly high-ceilinged space.

The entry is perpendicular to an equally long hall. We related the two by installing contemporary lanterns made by a metalsmith represented by Holly Hunt, a well-known design resource, throughout. We gave two halls their own distinct character by deploying different patterns.

As the owners wanted a fun entry, we placed Jeff Koons's white porcelain puppy, from Gagosian Gallery, on the red velvet console table (opposite). Here is a pure example of fantasy and function: Koons's dog doubles as a vase to hold big bunches of flowers. Since this is a pied-à-terre for a family who does not cook at home, we gathered take-out menus from the area's best restaurants and put them in a red leather album for their convenience (above).

Odegard made a shaped tone-on-tone beige runner that foreshortens the long hall. Its red binding picks up the color of the console. The American painter Yvonne Jacquette's aerial views of boats in a city harbor plays with your sense of perspective and injects still more color into the space. I bought this painting, *Hudson Crossings II* (2008), from D. C. Moore Gallery (opposite).

The clients wanted some whimsy, so on either side of the Swedish bench is a pair of witty surrealist sconces by Jean Cocteau that seem to say, "Need a light?" (right). The sconces were made famous in his 1946 movie *La Belle et la Bête*. Steve Perrault's meditative painting from Peter Findlay Gallery hangs above the bench.

COLORADO RANCH MUDROOM

olorado ranches in the wilderness, with all of their light, beauty, and vast open spaces, make them the ultimate luxury. The view to the west from this house showcases the Gore Range of snow-capped peaks. To the east, on a clear day, you can see all the way to Kansas. And directly south, contented cows munch on prairie grass with the light in the meadow constantly changing. To compliment the stone and pine mudroom, we assembled a collection of Swedish and Navaho rugs for the adjacent hallway.

The entry and door to this stone ranch house are made of simple pine (right). The mudroom is practical—there are sisal mats to absorb water from muddy cowboy boots, a built-in bench, and hooks for chaps and jackets (opposite).

FANTASY AND FUNCTION

Years ago, while visiting a friend in Ireland, I recall coming in from the gray damp of a typical Irish afternoon and stepping into an orange entrance hall. Since it rains constantly there, the Irish know how to make visitors feel warm and welcome. I decided right then that one day I would have an orange entry. While finishing the redo of my apartment, I was happy to discover that the color (a muskmelon shade) worked perfectly with the orange accents in the library and the mustardy golds of the living room, since both rooms are visible from the entry. Usually, the entry is the last space that designers address. We, in effect, "paint our way out of the house."

The art and furnishings marry function and utter whimsy, the old and the new, the very fine and flea market chic. In other words, the entry reflects the homeowner's personality—my tastes, appreciation, humor, and lineage. I don't give a fig where an object comes from as long as it works in the space.

One day I was looking at the entry and decided what I needed was an enormous, turquoise, Ultrasuede seashell backed with a mirror. That was my fantasy. So I called furniture maker Thomas Messel in London. The call started a fruitful collaborative design process on a special cabinet that fulfilled my fanciful aesthetic desire with some brass-tacks practicality. The baroque grotto design accommodates twelve sets of candlesticks and table decorations, like my collection of wire skyscrapers (right). In one of our countless emails, I expressed concern that the cabinet might not be "whoopie" enough. "Will it have enough studs?" I asked. To which Thomas replied, "Stephanie, it will have more studs than you'd find in a gay bar!"

Above the cabinet—which serves as a parking place for keys, mail, and packages—I hung a very fine French nineteenth-century water-gilded trumeau mirror that I bought at Sotheby's (opposite). By sheer luck, I found a flamboyant bust of Neptune at Lexington Gardens in New York. He's 2 feet tall, handsome, and wrapped in seashells—pure grotto extravagance. This entryway is all about juxtapositions. Here, the classical resides cheek by jowl with the whimsical.

Entryways are often storehouses for things with no other home. Recently, I inherited portraits of my great-grandparents, James and Olivia Phelps-Stokes, and hung them on the last available wall (opposite). James founded the Phelps Dodge mines in Arizona as well as an investment bank. In 1850, he commissioned the English artist Rand to paint their portraits. Here hang the two puritans, perhaps blushing a little at the adjacent entwined nude couple by Ron Cooper, a New Mexico–based artist. Yin-yang, the juxtaposition of old and new, is an important aspect of my design philosophy. The red ceiling fixture is a collapsible basket I picked up at the 26th Street flea market in New York, which I flipped over and converted into a chandelier.

Hall chairs come in many varieties. Mine are English nineteenth-century mahogany with splayed back legs and no seat upholstery. These small chairs have been strategically placed so that they don't scratch the walls. Guests can drop handbags, packages, shopping bags, and wet raincoats on them, and they are portable to make room for large dinner parties on Christmas and New Year's Eve.

ACKNOWLEDGMENTS

Some women do too much. Like me. So when a double knee replacement grounded me for half a year, I turned a disadvantage into an opportunity and wrote this book. I hope you will find it both inspiring and amusing. Since imitation is the best form of flattery, please use any and all ideas shown here to turn your own fantasies into practical realities.

Thank-yous are due to many. Jorge Arango took my verbal descriptions and turned them into prose. Every day we worked together we laughed and enjoyed his phenomenal home-cooked lunches. Since pictures make the book, my second thanks go to Michel Arnaud, for his patience documenting my work over the last ten years. Additional photography came from John Hall and Nancy Hall. We thought a few rooms would be more easily understood with schematics and, therefore, I asked Michael Harold, a recent graduate of New York School of Interior Design, to help. His drawings are as perfect as his bow ties!

Another wave of thanks goes to the team at Rizzoli: Sandy Gilbert, my editor—and now a great friend—for her intelligent guidance; Susi Oberhelman, for this wonderful layout; David Morton, for his constant encouragement; and finally to Charles Miers, a man of strong convictions, for believing in my project. Thanks also go to the rest of the excellent book team and copy editors at Rizzoli.

Two friends jumped in to edit. Wendy Moonan, a fellow Soaniac and writer for 1stdibs.com, did an early text edit. Jim Greenfield, a former editor of the *New York Times*, helped me rework the introduction.

The original inspiration for *Fantasy & Function* came from Kate Dyson of the Dining Room Shop in London. (She built the table on my book jacket!) Kate gave me the honorary title of "The Closet Queen," a moniker to describe my obsession with practicality. A second friend who urged me to write this book is Mindy Papp, owner of Florian Papp Antiques on Madison Avenue. Mindy has a great eye and a deep knowledge of furniture history and the decorative arts.

Many vendors deserve recognition. To cite just a few: Albert Menin Interiors, A. Schneller and Sons, Art in Construction, Penn & Fletcher, John Sullivan at Beauvais, and Tim Sheridan at Stark Carpets. A special thank-you goes to Benjamin Huntington, a talented architect who did the architectural drawings for many of the projects in this book.

But greatest thanks go to my former assistant, Louisa Ryan, and my Institute of Fine Arts classmate Michelle Brown, without whom none of this would have happened. This book has really been a collaboration, and they have been the most joyful helpers I could possibly imagine.

A special thank-you to all the clients who have given me the opportunities to bring functional reality to their fantasies, which have ranged from French Provençal and Japanese Zen to Moroccan exotic. Not only did my clients present me with fun, creative challenges, but they were also kind enough to let me photograph the results. Thank you all.

And a special last thank-you to my lifelong friend Xavier Guerrand-Hermès, for his generosity and beautifully written foreword.

CREDITS

All photography by Michel Arnaud with the exception of
John Hall: pages 156–157, 206–207, 208–209, 210, 211
Nancy Hill: pages 142, 150, 151, 152–153, 154, 155, 160, 162, 163, 164,
165, 200, 201, 202–203, 204, 205, 216, 217

Floor plans by Michael Harold: pages 23, 33, 177, 193
F J Hakimian provided the Persian rug made from antique dowry
pieces for the front jacket photograph.

Above: In a country kitchen, a pine side cabinet displays beautiful chartreuse French faïence.
Page 222: If you have twelve- or fourteen-foot ceilings, it's a wonderful opportunity to create a dramatic bed.
Here we hung a baldachin to emphasize the height of the room.